TICKET TO THE
NBA
FINALS

MARTIN GITLIN

ADMIT ONE

THE BIG GAME
YOUR FRONT ROW SEAT

45TH PARALLEL PRESS

Published in the United States of America by Cherry Lake Publishing Group
Ann Arbor, Michigan
www.cherrylakepublishing.com

Reading Adviser: Beth Walker Gambro, MS Ed., Reading Consultant, Yorkville, IL
Book Designer: Jen Wahi

Photo Credits: Cover: © Andre Ricardo/Dreamstime.com; page 5: © Martin Ellis /Dreamstime.com; page 7: © Sports
Images/Dreamstime.com; page 9: © Jerry Coli/Dreamstime.com; page 11: © Jerry Coli/Dreamstime.com; page 12:
© Jerry Coli/Dreamstime.com; page 17: © Jerry Coli/Dreamstime.com; page 19: © Jerry Coli/Dreamstime.com; page
21: © Jerry Coli/Dreamstime.com; page 22: © Sports Images/Dreamstime.com; page 25: © Jerry Coli/Dreamstime.com;
page 26: © Josh Kroese/Dreamstime.com; page 27: © Jerry Coli/Dreamstime.com; page 28 (top): © Cezary Dulniak/
Dreamstime.com; page 28 (bottom): © Dgareri/Dreamstime.com

45th Parallel Press is an imprint of Cherry Lake Publishing Group.

Library of Congress Cataloging-in-Publication Data

Names: Gitlin, Martin, author.
Title: Ticket to the NBA Finals / Martin Gitlin.
Description: Ann Arbor, Michigan : Cherry Lake Publishing, [2023] | Series:
  The big game | Audience: Grades 4-6 | Summary: "Who has won the NBA
  Finals? Who were the most valuable players? Written as high interest
  with struggling readers in mind, this series includes considerate
  vocabulary, engaging content and fascinating facts, clear text and
  formatting, and compelling photos. Educational sidebars include extra
  fun facts and information about each game. Includes table of contents,
  glossary, index, and author biography"-- Provided by publisher.
Identifiers: LCCN 2022039911 | ISBN 9781668919569 (hardcover) | ISBN
  9781668920589 (paperback) | ISBN 9781668921913 (ebook) | ISBN
  9781668923245 (pdf)
Subjects: LCSH: NBA Finals (Basketball)--History--Juvenile literature. |
  Basketball--United States--History--Juvenile literature. | National
  Basketball Association--History--Juvenile literature. |
  Basketball--Tournaments--United States--History--Juvenile literature.
Classification: LCC GV885.515.N37 G58 2023 | DDC
  796.323/640973--dc23/eng/20220901
LC record available at https://lccn.loc.gov/2022039911

Cherry Lake Publishing would like to acknowledge the work of the Partnership for 21st Century Learning, a network of
Battelle for Kids. Please visit http://www.battelleforkids.org/networks/p21

Printed in the United States of America
Corporate Graphics

Table of Contents

Introduction

The National Basketball Association (NBA) season starts in October. Every team plays 82 games. Those that win the most compete in the playoffs. That series of games decides the champion. Only 2 teams survive. They battle for the title.

The playoffs begin in April. The NBA Finals are played in June. It is a best-of-7 series. The first team to win 4 games takes the title. It is very exciting.

Rasheed Wallace played for the Detroit Pistons against the Boston Celtics. The Pistons and the Celtics are part of the NBA's Eastern Conference.

The NBA is divided into 2 sets of teams called conferences. Half play in the Eastern Conference. The others are in the Western Conference. Eight teams in each conference reach the playoffs.

The first 8 teams to win 4 games advance to the conference semifinals. The playoffs continue until 1 team remains from each conference. Those 2 play in the NBA Finals. It features the best players and teams ever.

Michael Jordan was one of the best basketball players of all time. He played for the Chicago Bulls.

A Super History

The NBA has changed greatly over the years. It began play in 1946 with 11 teams. It was then called the Basketball Association of America (BAA). Six teams made the playoffs.

The league had 30 teams in 2022. A total of 16 reached the playoffs.

The original BAA had no teams west of St. Louis. In 2022 it had 12. Four are in California.

The modern NBA has better athletes. They are quicker and faster. They jump higher. They shoot the ball more accurately.

Today the league is very popular. Millions more people watch the finals on TV. Fan attendance at all NBA games has increased greatly. Finals are always sold out.

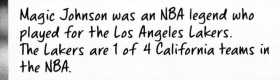

Magic Johnson was an NBA legend who played for the Los Angeles Lakers. The Lakers are 1 of 4 California teams in the NBA.

The top teams often rule the finals year after year. That is because they have the best players. A club that leads the NBA in wins for several seasons has a dynasty.

The first dynasty team was the Minneapolis Lakers. They won all but 1 title from 1949 to 1954. They had a superstar named George Mikan. He was 6 feet, 10 inches tall (208.28 centimeters).

Mikan was among the tallest players in the league. He led the NBA in scoring his first 3 seasons. He also led it twice in rebounds. A rebound is when a player grabs a missed shot.

No NBA team had a longer dynasty than Boston. The Celtics ruled basketball for 13 years. They won 11 titles from 1957 to 1969.

Two top rivals tried and failed to beat Boston. A rival is a person or team that competes with another to be the best. The first was St. Louis. The Hawks lost 3 finals to the Celtics. The other was the Los Angeles Lakers. That was after the team moved from Minneapolis. They lost to the Celtics 6 times from 1962 to 1969.

The NBA kept adding teams in the 1960s and 1970s. It had grown to 17 in 1970. By that time the Boston dynasty was over.

Reggie Lewis (35) and Larry Bird (33) played for the Boston Celtics. The Celtics had an NBA dynasty.

One rivalry in the late 1970s created great interest.

The NBA suffered in the late 1970s. Fewer fans were coming to games. TV ratings were down.

That all changed in 1979. That's when the NBA had 2 amazing rookies. Those are first-year players. One was Larry Bird. He played for the Celtics. The other was Earvin "Magic" Johnson. He joined the Lakers.

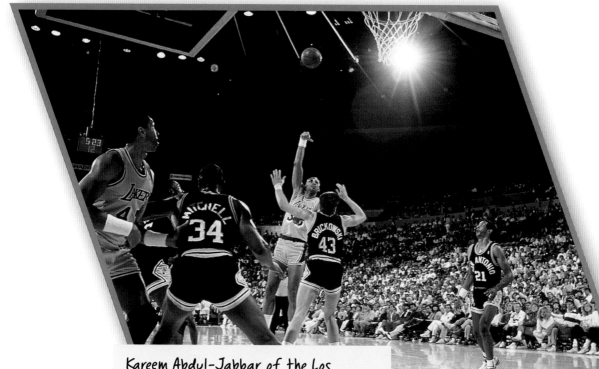

Kareem Abdul-Jabbar of the Los Angeles Lakers shoots his sky hook shot.

★ Basketball is different from other sports. Each team has only 5 players on the court at once. That means 1 player can turn an average team into a champion.

★ Perhaps the best example was Lew Alcindor. He later changed his name to Kareem Abdul-Jabbar. He joined a losing Milwaukee Bucks team in 1969. He turned them into a winner. Soon he led them to a title.

★ The 7 feet, 2 inch (218.44 centimeters) tall center owned the deadliest shot in basketball history. Nobody could block his sky hook. That is a shot taken with a looping motion.

LEGENDS
OF THE SPORT

Their talents drove their teams into the finals year after year. Either the Lakers or the Celtics played in 10 straight finals. They faced each other 3 times. Boston beat Los Angeles in 1984. The Lakers defeated the Celtics in 1985 and 1987.

A new superstar soon led his team to greatness. His name was Michael Jordan. His Chicago Bulls won 6 NBA titles from 1991 to 1998. He is widely considered the greatest player ever.

Other stars began to shine in the 2000s. They led their teams to many NBA Finals and titles. Among them was Kobe Bryant. He led the Lakers to 3 straight NBA titles. Bryant was a scoring machine. His team lost just 3 Finals games from 2000 to 2002.

Superstars continued to lead super teams. Among them was Golden State guard Steph Curry. Some believe he is the greatest shooter of all time. He led the Warriors to championships in 2015, 2017, 2018, and 2022.

Curry's main rival those seasons was Cleveland forward LeBron James. Many people think James is the best player ever. The Cavaliers played Golden State in 4 straight finals. But they only won in 2016.

☆ Some called them dirty. Others felt they just played rough. They were the Detroit Pistons. They won NBA titles in 1989 and 1990.

☆ The Pistons had tough players. They played the best defense in the league. They sometimes got into fights on the court.

☆ The players some called dirty were Dennis Rodman and Bill Laimbeer. Detroit also boasted a great point guard. His name was Isiah Thomas.

WAY BACK WHEN

Early Days, Big Moments

The rivalry between Larry Bird and Magic Johnson was magic. But an earlier one was just as exciting.

Bill Russell played center for the Celtics. Russell was perhaps the best defensive player ever.

His rival was Wilt Chamberlain. He played for the Warriors and Lakers. He was a bit taller than Russell. And he was an offensive force. Chamberlain averaged an amazing 50 points per game in 1962.

The 2 players met often in the playoffs. Both played well. But the Celtics dominated those battles. Russell and Chamberlain met twice in the NBA Finals. Boston won in both 1964 and 1969.

Bill Russell of the Boston Celtics jumps up to get the ball.

The Lakers–Celtics finals were exciting. They featured amazing talent. Among them was Lakers guard Jerry West. He made one of the greatest plays ever. It was Game 3 of the 1962 NBA Finals. West stole the ball and scored to win the game.

But Boston won the series. Russell was the hero. He had 30 points and an amazing 40 rebounds.

Some believe Game 5 of the 1976 finals was the best ever. It was between the Celtics and the Phoenix Suns. It had many strange and exciting moments.

The game was tied after 48 minutes. So it went into overtime. That is extra time played to decide a winner. The game still was tied after the first overtime. So it went into a second overtime and then a third overtime!

The Celtics led by 1 point in the third overtime. But Suns forward Curtis Perry hit a shot with 5 seconds left. That put his team ahead.

Boston superstar John Havlicek came to the rescue. He made a shot as time ran out. That gave the Celtics the win. They went on to win the series.

John Havlicek of the Boston Celtics helped his team win against the Suns with his final shot.

The Next Generation

The 1970s had many epic finals battles. The best may have been in 1977. It featured 2 of the game's greatest players.

One was Julius "Dr. J" Erving. He played for the Philadelphia 76ers. The other was Bill Walton of the Portland Trail Blazers.

Both played great. But Walton led his team to the title. He was amazing in Game 6. He scored 20 points. He had 23 rebounds. He added 7 assists. Those are passes that lead to baskets. He even blocked 8 shots.

Those numbers were incredible. But those of Magic Johnson 3 years later were better.

Bill Walton led the Portland Trail Blazers to win the NBA Finals in 1977.

Michael Jordan goes in for a layup. A layup is a 2-point shot. Players use one hand to bounce the ball off the backboard and into the net.

Johnson was a point guard. But he was forced to play center in 1980. That was because Kareem Abdul-Jabbar was hurt.

Many believe the finest NBA player ever was Michael Jordan. Perhaps his greatest moment came in Game 6 of the 1998 finals.

That was when the Bulls battled Utah. The Jazz led by 3 points. There were just 41 seconds left in the game.

First Jordan scored on a layup. In this shot, the player uses one hand to bounce the ball off the backboard and into the basket. Then Jordan stole the ball from Jazz star Karl Malone. He drove to the basket and stopped quickly. Jordan finished the job by hitting a long shot. He had scored 45 points to give the Bulls another title. It was their sixth title in 8 years.

New York Knicks center Willis Reed had a torn thigh muscle. There seemed no way he could play Game 7 of the 1970 finals.

The Knicks were about to play the Lakers. The title was on the line. And the great center limped onto the court. He got huge cheers from the fans.

Reed wanted to inspire his team to victory. And the Knicks did win. They were league champions. But they haven't won a championship since.

AMAZING MOMENT

Into the 2000s

Big finals moments aren't always about superstars. Often other players have come up big. One example was Robert Horry. He played for several teams. And he made big shots in the NBA Finals.

In 2005 Horry was playing for the San Antonio Spurs. It was Game 5 against Detroit. The game went into overtime. Horry dunked the ball for a key basket. Then he nailed a long shot worth 3 points. That won the game.

Two games later, the Spurs were world champions. And they had Horry to thank for it.

Another exciting moment was in 2013. It was Game 6 of the NBA Finals. San Antonio needed a win to stay alive. Miami was trying to win the series.

Robert Horry played for many teams in the NBA. Here he is playing for the Houston Rockets.

The Heat were down by 3 points. They looked doomed. But Miami guard Ray Allen got the ball. He was among the best shooters in NBA history. And he hit a 3-pointer at the buzzer.

His team won in overtime. And they took Game 7 for the title.

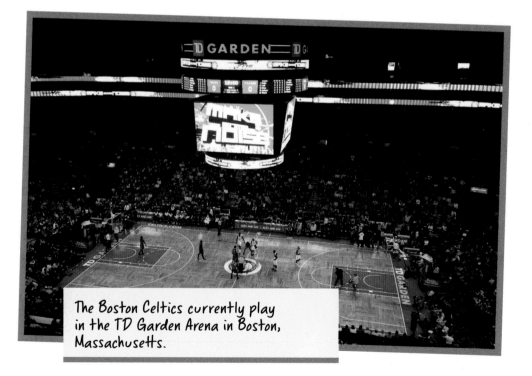

The Boston Celtics currently play in the TD Garden Arena in Boston, Massachusetts.

Kobe Bryant won 5 NBA championships with the Los Angeles Lakers. He was the youngest player to ever start in an NBA game. He passed away in 2020.

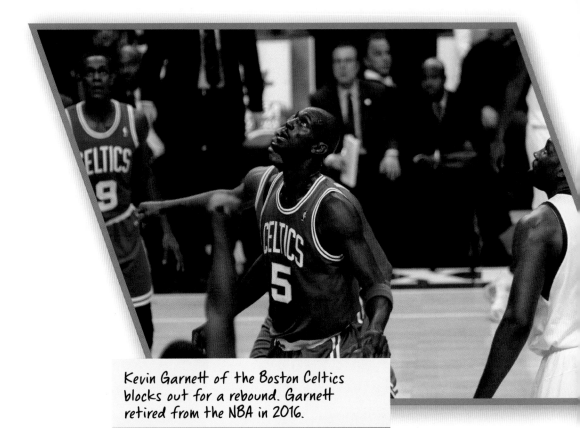

Kevin Garnett of the Boston Celtics blocks out for a rebound. Garnett retired from the NBA in 2016.

Lebron James has played in the NBA finals 10 times. Here he plays against the Toronto Raptors for his then team, Miami Heat.

The Celtics have won 17 titles through 2022.

 The Lakers have also won 17 NBA titles.

 The Warriors are next on the list. But they are far behind. They have won 7 championships.

A BIT OF TRIVIA

Activity

Go online and read about your favorite NBA team. Learn about the charity work it does. Find out how it helps people in its city. Then ask your teacher if you can write about it.

Learn More

BOOKS

Anderson, Kirsten. *Who Is Michael Jordan?* New York: Penguin Workshop, 2019.

Curcio, Anthony. *Stephen Curry: The Children's Book: The Boy Who Never Gave Up*. CreateSpace Independent Publishing Platform, 2016.

Gitlin, Marty. *NBA: Underdog Stories*. Minneapolis, MN: ABDO Publishing, 2018.

WEBSITES

Jr. NBA: https://jr.nba.com

Kiddle: Basketball Facts for Kids: https://kids.kiddle.co/Basketball

Sports Illustrated Kids—Basketball: https://www.sikids.com/basketball

Glossary

assists (uh-SISTS) passes that leads to a basket

attendance (uh-TEN-duhns) number of fans at a game

conferences (KAHN-fuh-ruhn-sez) two groups of teams into which the NBA is divided

dynasty (DYE-nuh-stee) period in which the same team wins many titles

hook (HUHK) sweeping shot from over the head

layup (LAY-uhp) shot taken next to the basket and banked off the backboard

overtime (OH-vuhr-tym) extra period of play in a game

playoffs (PLAY-awfs) series of games that determine NBA Finals

rebounds (REE-bowndz) balls grabbed after a missed shot

rivals (RYE-vuhlz) people or teams that compete with each other to be the best

rookies (RUH-keez) first-year players

Index

About the Author

Marty Gitlin is a sports book author based in Cleveland. He won more than 45 awards as a newspaper sportswriter from 1991 to 2002. Included was a first-place award from the Associated Press for his coverage of the 1995 World Series. He has had more than 200 books published since 2006. Most of them were written for students.